PEACE

PEACE

PEACE

和平

سَلامٌ سَلامٌ سَلامٌ سَلامٌ

和平

和平

I0410772

PAIX PAZ

PAIX PAZ

PAIX PAZ

PEACE

PEACE

PEACE

和平 سَلامٌ سَلامٌ سَلامٌ سَلامٌ

和平

和平

PAIX PAZ

PAIX PAZ

PAIX PAZ

Peace, Peace, Peace: A Peace Coloring Book from
Around the World

Written and Illustrated by Karen Porter

Copyright 2003 pawprintpress

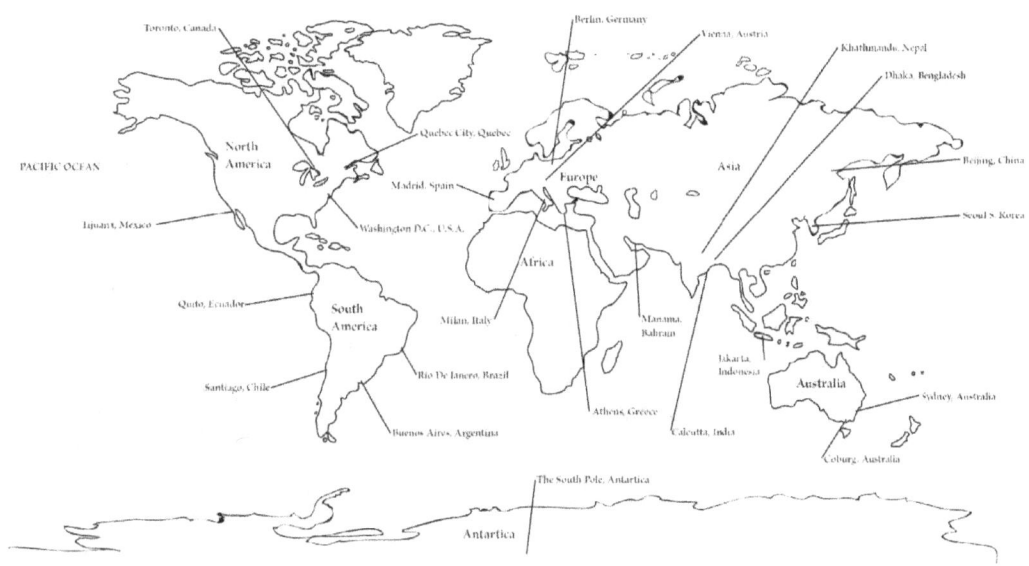

On March 15, 2003 Over 11 million
people gathered in over 120 countries
around the world to demonstrate their
love of peace. These demonstrations were
made to bring the spirit of
understanding, tolerance, and friendship
to all neighborhoods around the world.
As you color these pages remember that
we can have universal peace and
brotherhood.

We marched
in the
streets.

2

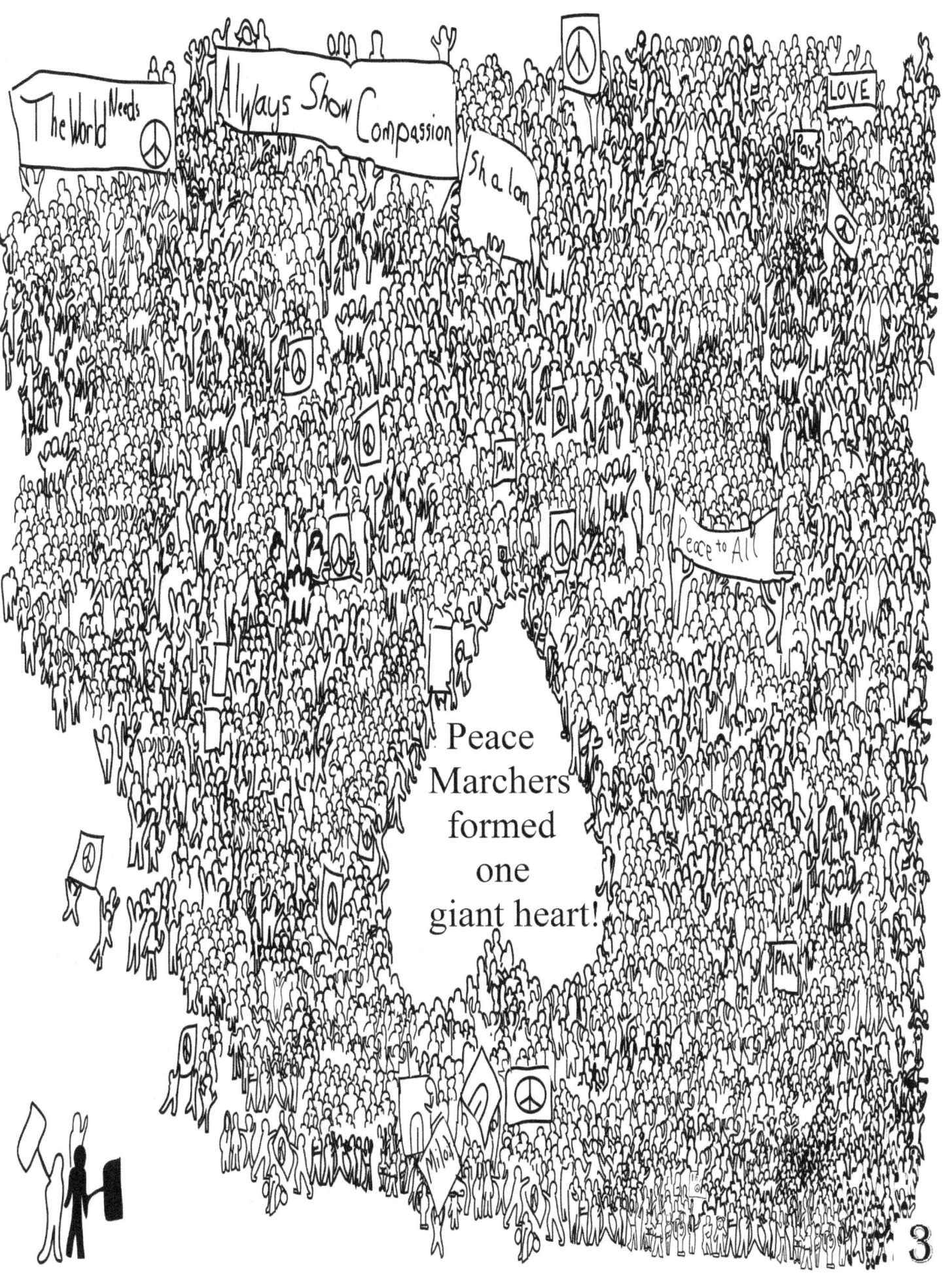

We stood in the street with signs for peace with warm hats on our heads.

4.

We walked banners down streets with palm trees in the breeze.

5.

We held hands together in snowy cold lands.

6.

We met peace on the golden shore.

We came together with flags from all countries to show we were united in peace for our world.

8.

We held flags for peace.

We held
flowers
for
Peace!

10.

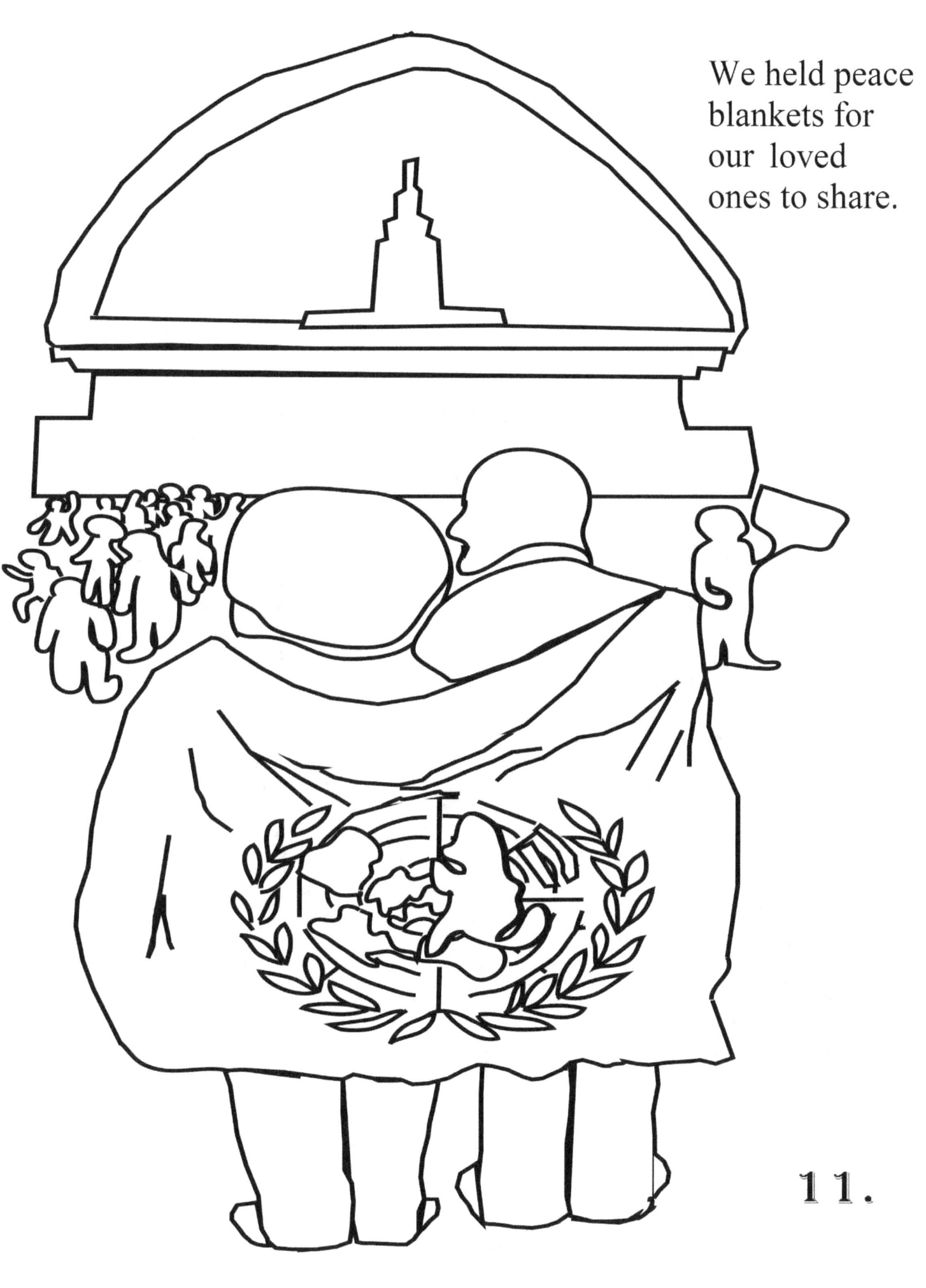

We held peace
blankets for
our loved
ones to share.

11.

OXI
ΠOΛEMO
ΣTO IPAK

We made
our faces,
faces of
peace.

12.

We made doves for peace.

13.

We made banners for peace.

We wrote signs on the street for peace.

15.

We drummed drums to bring peace for all.

16.

We drummed
drums for
peace on the
Washington
mall.

17.

We lit
candles for
our loved
ones for
peace
remembering
our losses
from war
after
war.

18.

We lit candles of hope for ending all war.

19.

20. We lit candles for peace and wrote peace on our face and clothes.

We lit candles in groups and we sang for peace from our hearts.

21.

We held our hands in peace signs with our friends from school.

22.

We wore hats
for peace and
held our
hands in
peace signs.

23.

Soft whispers and loud shouts. We all need to learn what peace is about.

We flew ribbons in the air.

We held signs on
shoulders to
answer the call.

North,
south,
east,
west,
small
and tall
peace
needs us
all.

Anti War

MEDICARE NOT MISSILES

Coburg Rally
15 March 2003

27.

These illustrations are taken from actual pictures of peace marchers on March 15, 2003. Can you guess where in the world these pictures are from?

Madrid Spain: Hundreds of thousands of protestors gathered in streets with signs that filled block after block after block and disrupted traffic for many hours.

Tell Aviv, Israel: Israelis and Palestinians held a rally together against a war with Iraq in Tel Aviv. marching in our thousands down the wide Ibn Gvirol Street; a living forest of colorful banners and placards and hand-painted signs, Jews and Arabs together with slogans chanted alternately in both languages and occasionally in English; reaching the Museum Plaza for a prolonged rally, with speakers addressing the crowd from the steps of the Public Library

Vienna, Austria: Throngs of peace demonstrators gathered in square after town square. This group created a space in the middle of their assembly that formed a heart.

Montreal, Canada: The warm woolen hats stood out as the masses of caring hearts withstood subzero temperatures to make our voices be heard.

Rio De Janero, Brazil: The palm trees blew in the breeze as protestors gathered in streets with banners in many Brazilian cities. This is just one town.

The South Pole: A group of international scientists, comprising citizens from all over the world, gathered in a circle to show the world that they too believed in peace.

Sydney, Australia: Australians held vigils, picnics, education sessions and marches. One brave soul placed a sign saying "no war" on the top most perch in the harbor.

Athens, Greece: This man has painted a peace sign on his face. He was one among hundreds of thousands of peace protestors that filled city streets.

Milan, Italy: People representing every nation on earth came together carrying flags of all different nationalities asking the world to come together to stop war.

Quebec City, Canada: Hundreds of thousands of marchers met to protest the war carrying flags of their own nations. This woman carries the flag of Quebec, Canada.

Jakarta, Indonesia: The flower is a symbol of peace and love in Jakarta. Thousands of women lined the streets with flowers in their hands.

Berlin, Germany: This couple draped a blue United Nations flag over themselves as they watched the hundreds of thousands of protestors march through Berlin.

Seoul, South Korea: Here is one peace activist and his dove. Thousands more people threw paper doves into the evening sky in downtown Seoul.

Buenos Aires, Argentina: People met to make signs and banners. These girls from Argentina are making a banner of a newspaper and a sheet.

Beijing, China: Many people in China gathered around newspaper boards leaving their own messages calling for an end to war with Iraq

Katmandu, Napal: Drummers gathered in streets to sound out their objection to the war. Speeches were given and protesters were heard.

Washington D.C., United States:
Hundreds of thousands of marchers met on the Washington Mall.

Manama, Bahrain: Women held candles in honor of the witnesses against war that had been killed. They mourned the loss of their fathers, brothers, and sons.

Calcutta, India: Candlelight vigils were held in over one thousand cities across the world. These women came together as a strong force in India. They carried candles, sang songs and prayed to stop the war.

Berlin, Germany: Young girls from school met together to hold a banner in front of historic downtown Berlin buildings.

Toronto, Canada: A boy holds his hand high with a peace symbol as he sports his newly made peace hat.

Dhaka, Bangladesh: This young boy wearing a traditional turban also holds his hand high asking to end the suffering war has caused.

Tijuana, Mexico: These young students from school are with their teacher who is a Catholic Nun. They are waving ribbons for peace.

Panama City, Panama: This child rides high on her father's shoulders. She is among the many who marched in Panama.

Coburg, Australia: This young child is helping his mom display a sign. He was part of the many marches, demonstrations, educational sessions and rallies Australia had.

Worldwide protests were held against the war on Iraq. Some thought war was inevitable. Others clung to the hope that they could slow or stop it. Either way, we joined around the world on March 15, 2003 in an outpouring of our vision for peace. The cries against war were everywhere.

We believed we could make a difference. We traveled great distances to challenge the march toward war and Bush's justifications for it. We wanted the world to know this was not being done in our name. Candlelight prayer gatherings were planned in a series of vigils in more than 1,000 cities around the world. In Stockholm, Germany speakers rallied. In Baghdad we protested. In Cypress, Greece we marched. In downtown Seoul, South Korea we threw paper doves into the evening sky. In Traralgon, Australia we demonstrated. In Melbourne, Australia we held vigils, picnics, education sessions and marches. In Moscow we demonstrated and rallied, waving red flags. In Bangkok we rallied and listened to anti-war speeches. In London we organized and marched through central London. In Arabia, Turkey, Syria, Egypt, Qatar and Pakistan we rallied in support of peace. In Bucharest Romania we marched through the capital.

People rallied worldwide, in some cases pressing close to symbols of U.S. power: the Washington Monument and the White House in Washington, the U.S. air base in Frankfurt, Germany, and U.S. embassies in Greece and Cyprus. They also took to the streets throughout Europe, Asia and the Middle East. We pray that some day in our lifetimes our voices will be heard.

30.

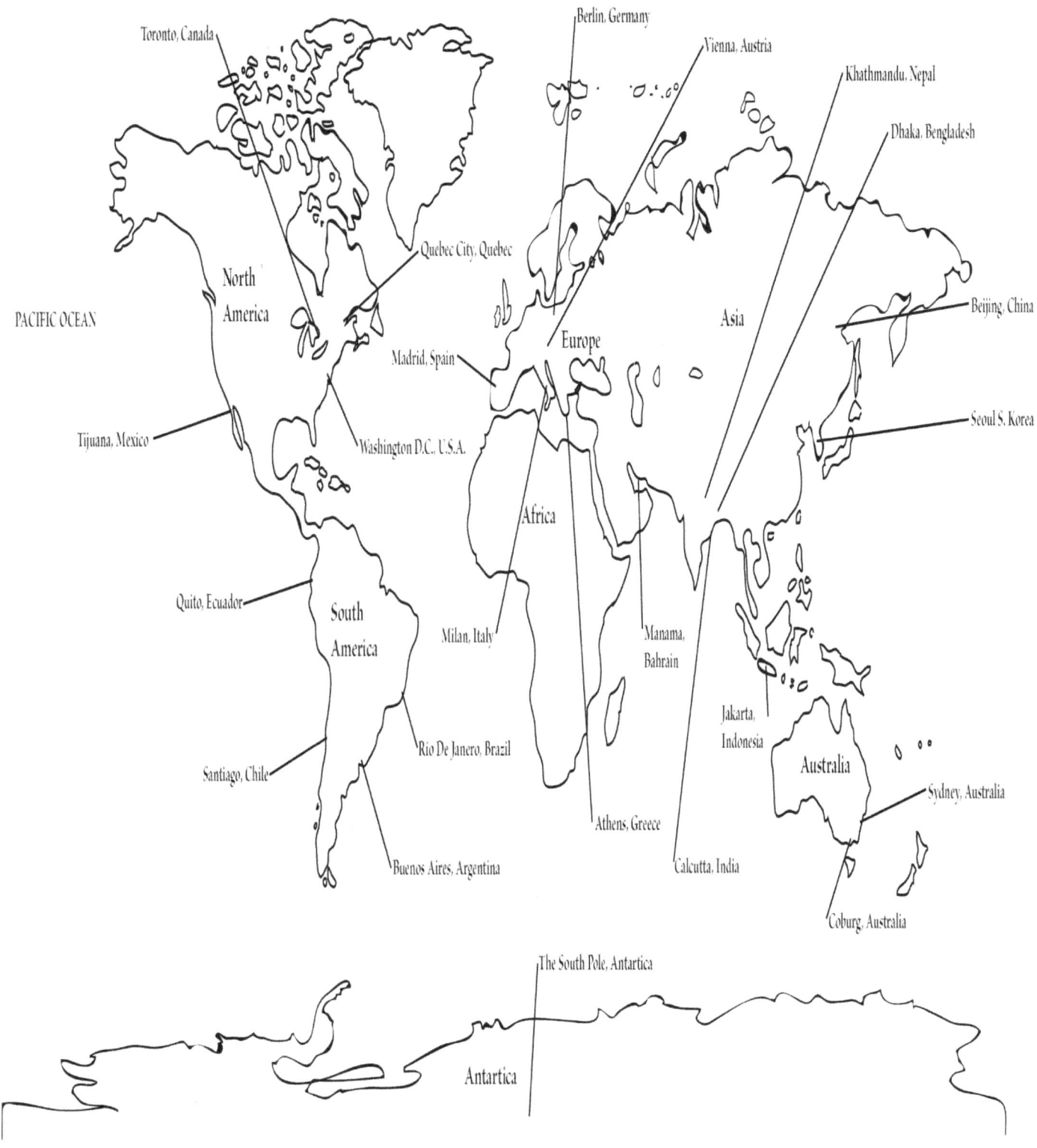

My prayer for humanity is that we can all join together to peacefully protect our planet for all people everywhere.

www.ingramcontent.com/pod-product-compliance
Lightning Source LLC
Chambersburg PA
CBHW081807280526
45789CB00008B/3041